PIANO SOLO

OPERA AT THE MOVIES

ISBN 0-7935-2246-3

Hal Leonard Publishing Corporation
7777 West Bluemound Road P.O. Box 13819 Milwaukee, WI 53213

Copyright © 1993 by HAL LEONARD PUBLISHING CORPORATION
International Copyright Secured   All Rights Reserved

For all works contained herein:
Unauthorized copying, arranging, adapting, recording or public performance is an infringement of copyright.
Infringers are liable under the law.

EVANSTON PUBLIC LIBRARY
1703 ORRINGTON AVENUE
EVANSTON, ILLINOIS 60201

OPERA AT THE MOVIES

CONTENTS

AMADEUS *The Marriage of Figaro*	Wolfgang Amadeus Mozart	"Contessa, perdono"	4
		"Ecco la marcia"	5
APOCALYPSE NOW *Die Walküre*	Richard Wagner	"Ride of the Valkyries"	8
BABETTE'S FEAST *Don Giovanni*	Wolfgang Amadeus Mozart	"Là ci darem la mano"	12
BREAKING AWAY *Martha*	Friedrich von Flotow	"M'appari, tutt' amor"	17
CARMEN *Carmen*	Georges Bizet	"Habañera"	20
		"Seguidilla"	22
		"Toreador Song"	26
CHARIOTS OF FIRE *The Mikado*	G. S. Gilbert & Arthur Sullivan	"Three Little Maids"	32
DIVA *La Wally*	Alfredo Catalani	"Ebben, n'andro lontano"	29
FATAL ATTRACTION *Madama Butterfly*	Giacomo Puccini	"Un bel dì vedremo"	34
FOUL PLAY *The Mikado*	G. S. Gilbert & Arthur Sullivan	"If You Want to Know Who We Are"	38
GODFATHER III *Cavalleria Rusticana*	Pietro Mascagni	"Intermezzo"	41
HANNAH AND HER SISTERS *Manon Lescaut*	Giacomo Puccini	"Sola, perduta, abbandonata"	44
MOONSTRUCK *La Bohème*	Giacomo Puccini	"Quando men vo"	48
		"O soave fanciulla"	50
		"Che gelida manina"	52
A NIGHT AT THE OPERA *Il Trovatore*	Giuseppe Verdi	"The Anvil Chorus"	56
PARADISE *The Magic Flute*	Wolfgang Amadeus Mozart	"Queen of the Night's Vengeance Aria"	66
PRETTY WOMAN *La Traviata*	Giuseppe Verdi	"Addio, del passato"	58
A ROOM WITH A VIEW *Gianni Schicchi*	Giacomo Puccini	"O mio babbino caro"	60
		"Firenze è come un albero fiorito"	62
La Rondine	Giacomo Puccini	"La Canzone di Doretta"	71
THE UNTOUCHABLES *I Pagliacci*	Ruggero Leoncavallo	"Vesti la giubba"	76
WALL STREET *Rigoletto*	Giuseppe Verdi	"Questo e quella"	74

AMADEUS
Contessa, perdono
from *Le Nozze di Figaro*

W. A. Mozart

AMADEUS

Ecco la marcia
from *Le Nozze di Figaro*

Moderate march

W. A. Mozart

APOCALYPSE NOW

Ride of the Valkyries
from *Die Walküre*

Richard Wagner

Copyright © 1993 by HAL LEONARD PUBLISHING CORPORATION
International Copyright Secured. All Rights Reserved

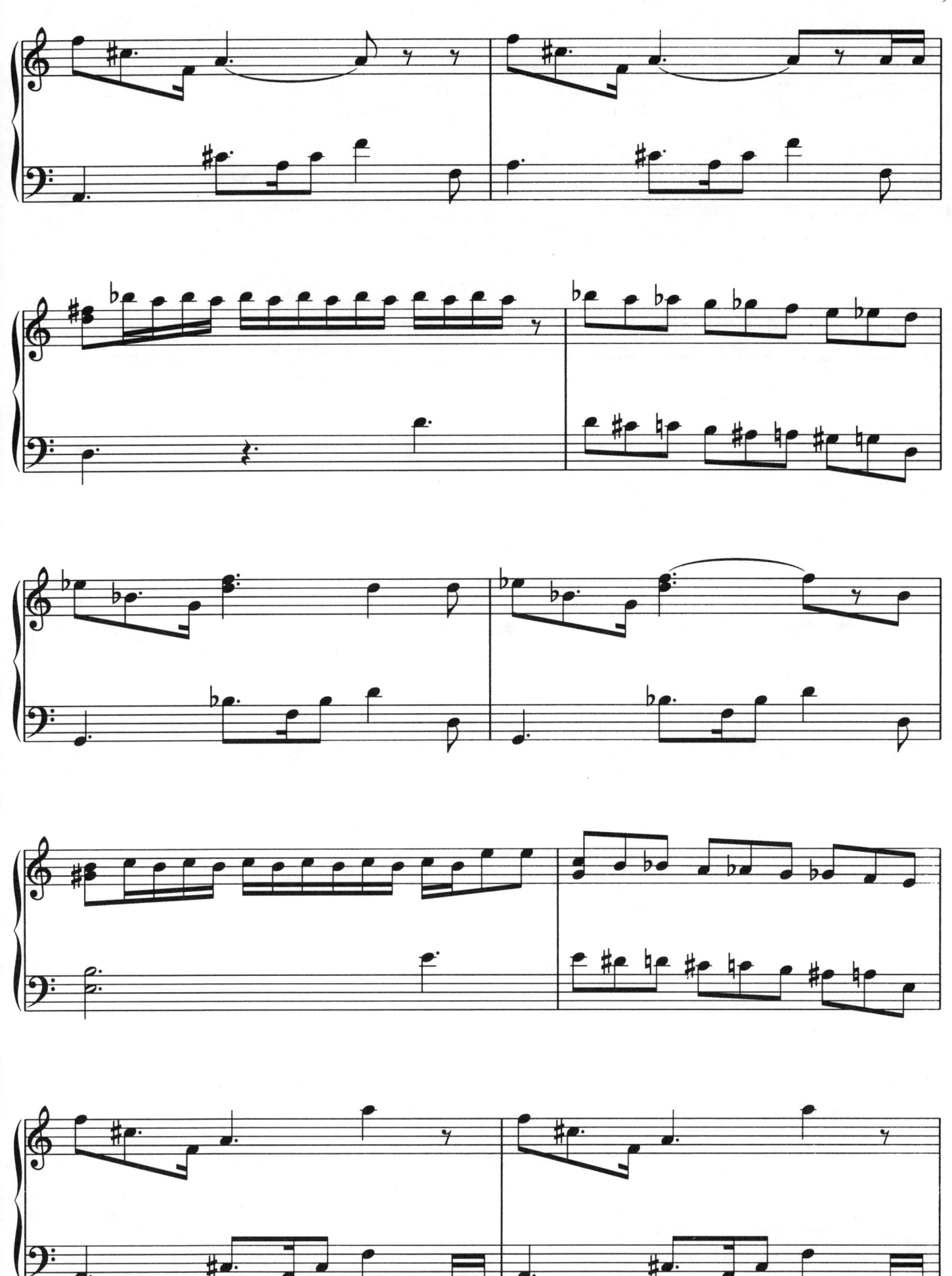

BABETTE'S FEAST

Là ci darem la mano
from *Don Giovanni*

Andante

W. A. Mozart

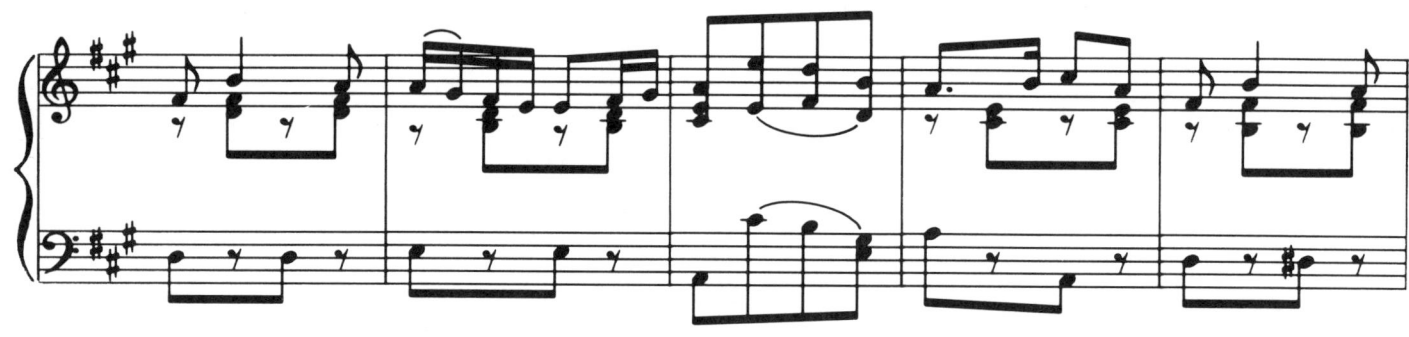

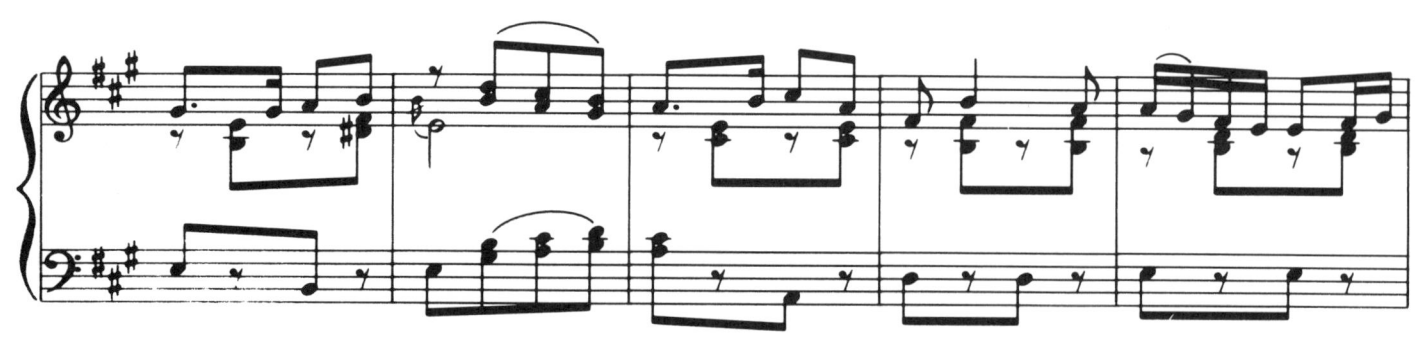

Copyright © 1993 by HAL LEONARD PUBLISHING CORPORATION
International Copyright Secured.   All Rights Reserved

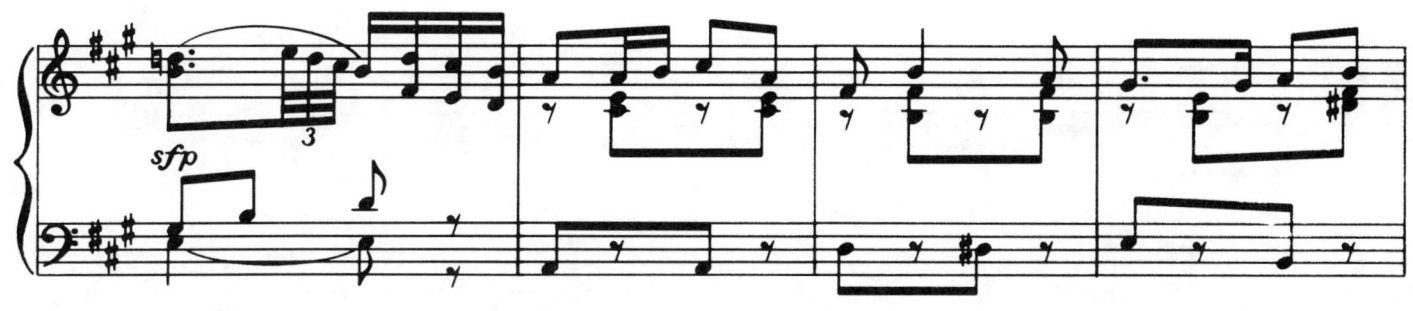

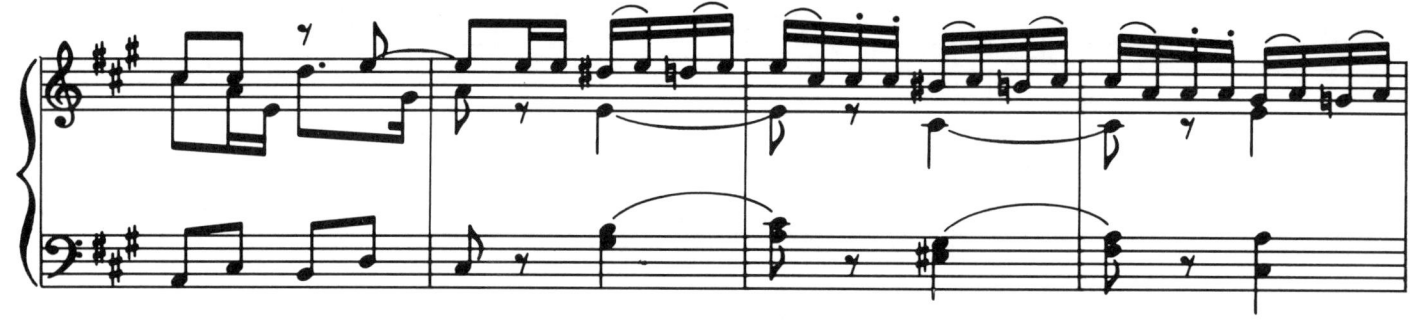

Allegro

BREAKING AWAY

M'appari tutt'amor
(Ach, so fromm)
from *Martha*

Friedrich von Flotow

Allegro moderato

Copyright © 1993 by HAL LEONARD PUBLISHING CORPORATION
International Copyright Secured. All Rights Reserved.

CARMEN

Habañera
from *Carmen*

Georges Bizet

Copyright © 1993 by HAL LEONARD PUBLISHING CORPORATION
International Copyright Secured. All Rights Reserved.

CARMEN

Seguidilla

from *Carmen*

Georges Bizet

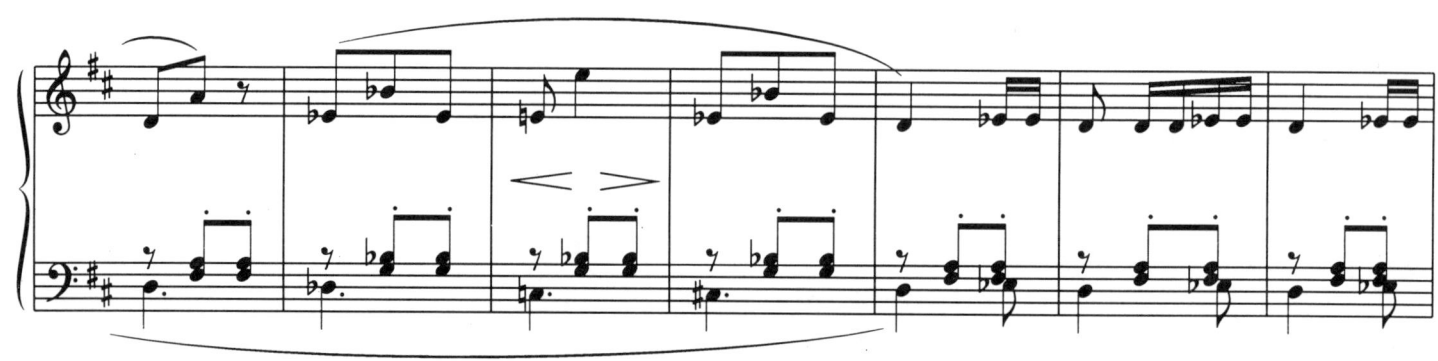

CARMEN
Toreador Song
from *Carmen*

Allegro moderato

Georges Bizet

Copyright © 1993 by HAL LEONARD PUBLISHING CORPORATION
International Copyright Secured. All Rights Reserved.

DIVA

Ebben, n'andrò lontana
from *La Wally*

Alfredo Catalani

CHARIOTS OF FIRE

Three Little Maids
from *The Mikado*

G.S. Gilbert
& Arthur Sullivan

Copyright © 1993 by HAL LEONARD PUBLISHING CORPORATION
International Copyright Secured. All Rights Reserved

FATAL ATTRACTION

Un bel dì vedremo
from *Madama Butterfly*

Giacomo Puccini

FOUL PLAY
If You Want to Know Who We Are
from *The Mikado*

Arthur Sullivan

Copyright © 1993 by HAL LEONARD PUBLISHING CORPORATION
International Copyright Secured. All Rights Reserved.

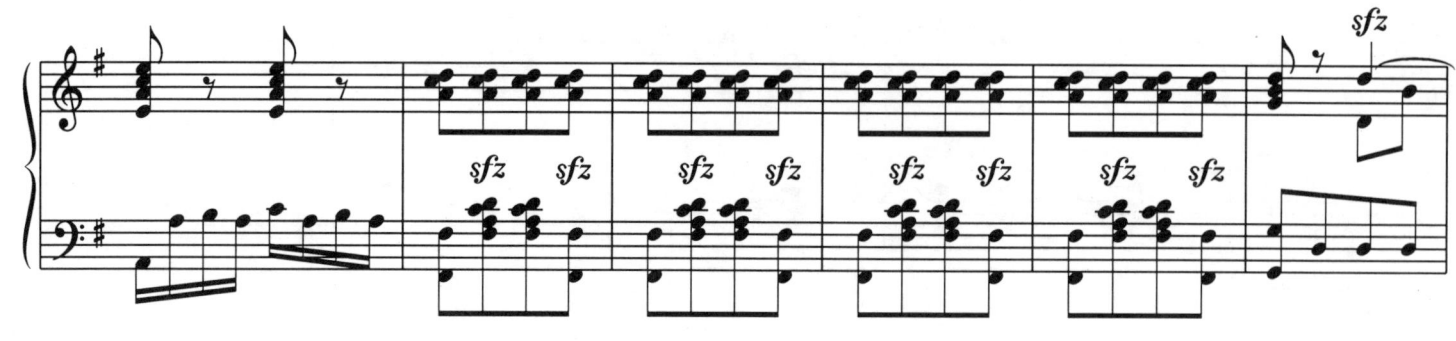

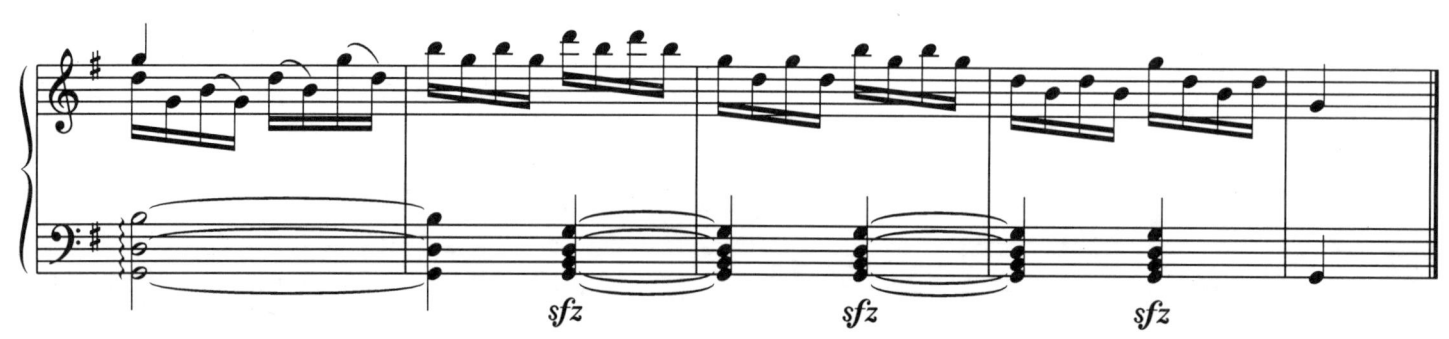

THE GODFATHER III

Intermezzo
from *Cavalleria Rusticana*

Pietro Mascagni

HANNAH AND HER SISTERS

Sola, perduta, abbandonata
from *Manon Lescaut*

Giacomo Puccini

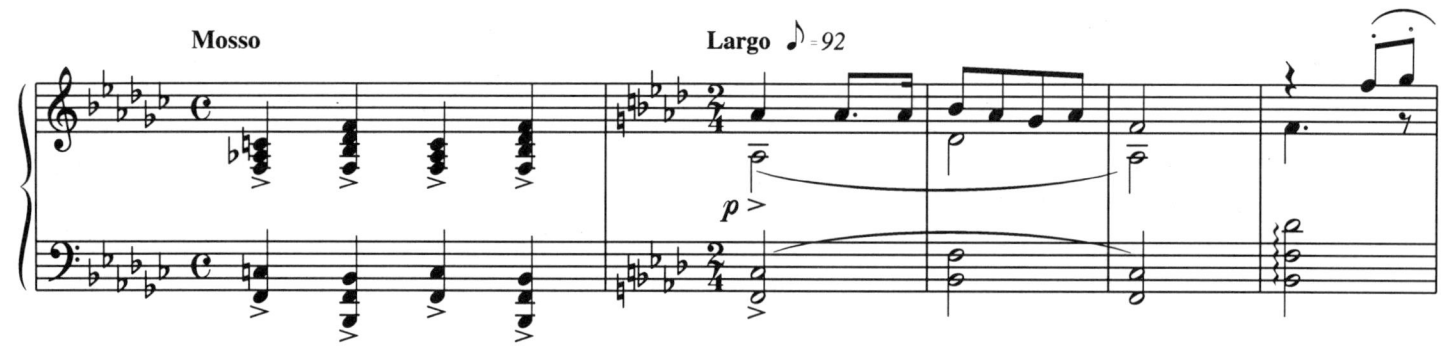

Copyright © 1993 by HAL LEONARD PUBLISHING CORPORATION
International Copyright Secured. All Rights Reserved.

MOONSTRUCK

Quando men vo
from *La Bohème*

Waltz in steady tempo

Giacomo Puccini

Copyright © 1993 by HAL LEONARD PUBLISHING CORPORATION
International Copyright Secured. All Rights Reserved

MOONSTRUCK

O soave fanciulla
from *La Bohème*

Giacomo Puccini

* *Bring out melody*

Copyright © 1993 by HAL LEONARD PUBLISHING CORPORATION
International Copyright Secured. All Rights Reserved

MOONSTRUCK

Che gelida manina
from *La Bohème*

Giacomo Puccini

Copyright © 1993 by HAL LEONARD PUBLISHING CORPORATION
International Copyright Secured. All Rights Reserved

A NIGHT AT THE OPERA

The Anvil Chorus
from *Il Trovatore*

Giuseppe Verdi

PRETTY WOMAN

Addio, del passato
from *La Traviata*

Giuseppe Verdi

Copyright © 1993 by HAL LEONARD PUBLISHING CORPORATION
International Copyright Secured. All Rights Reserved.

A ROOM WITH A VIEW

O mio babbino caro
from *Gianni Schicchi*

Giacomo Puccini

A ROOM WITH A VIEW

Firenze è come un albero fiorito
from *Gianni Schicchi*

Giacomo Puccini

Andante mosso un po' sostenuto ♩= 92
(ad uso di stornello toscano)

Copyright © 1993 by HAL LEONARD PUBLISHING CORPORATION
International Copyright Secured. All Rights Reserved.

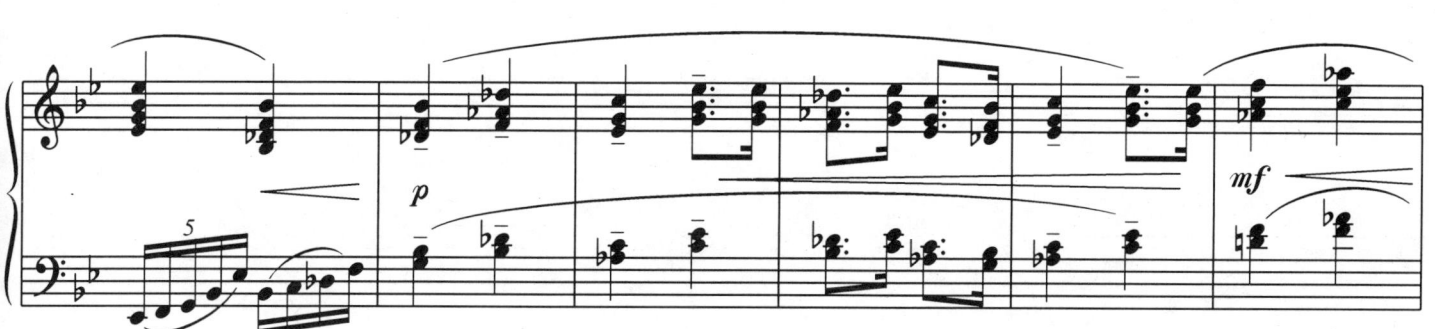

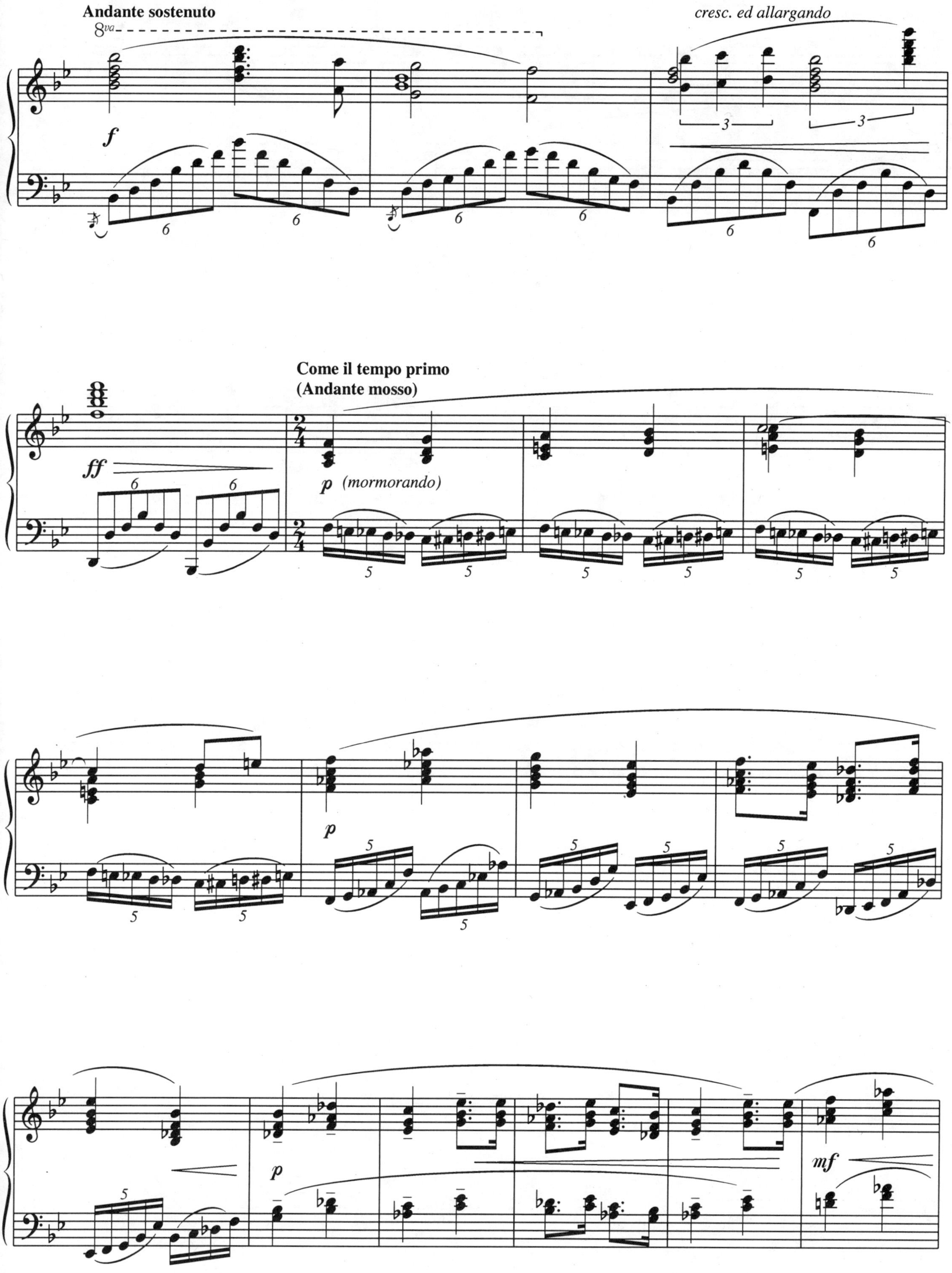
Andante sostenuto
8va
f
cresc. ed allargando
3
3
6
6
6
6
6
6
ff
6
6
Come il tempo primo
(Andante mosso)
2
4
p
(mormorando)
5
p
mf

64

Un po' sostenuto

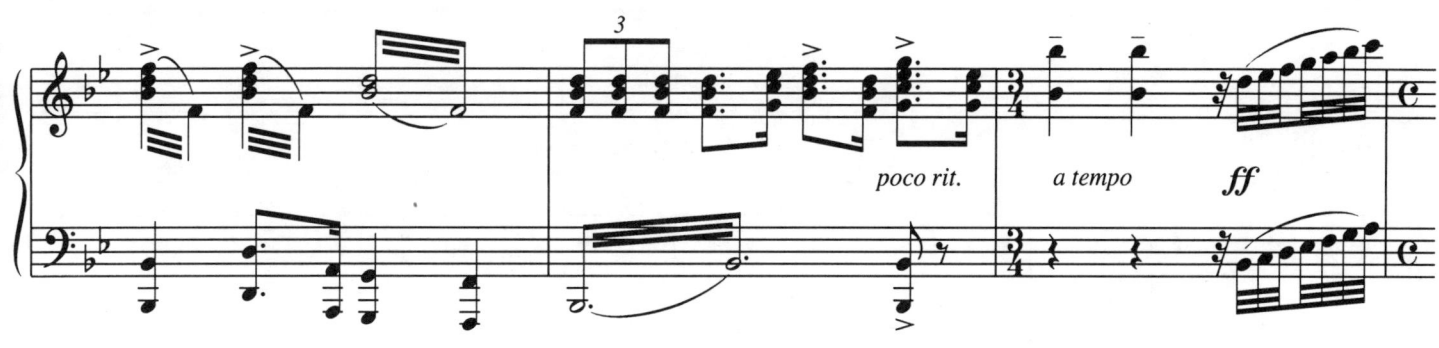

PARADISE

Queen of the Night's Vengeance Aria
from *The Magic Flute*

W. A. Mozart

A ROOM WITH A VIEW
La Canzone di Doretta
from *La Rondine*

Giacomo Puccini

Copyright © 1993 by HAL LEONARD PUBLISHING CORPORATION
International Copyright Secured. All Rights Reserved.

WALL STREET
Questa o quella
from *Rigoletto*

Giuseppe Verdi

THE UNTOUCHABLES

Vesti la giubba
from I Pagliacci

Ruggiero Leoncavallo

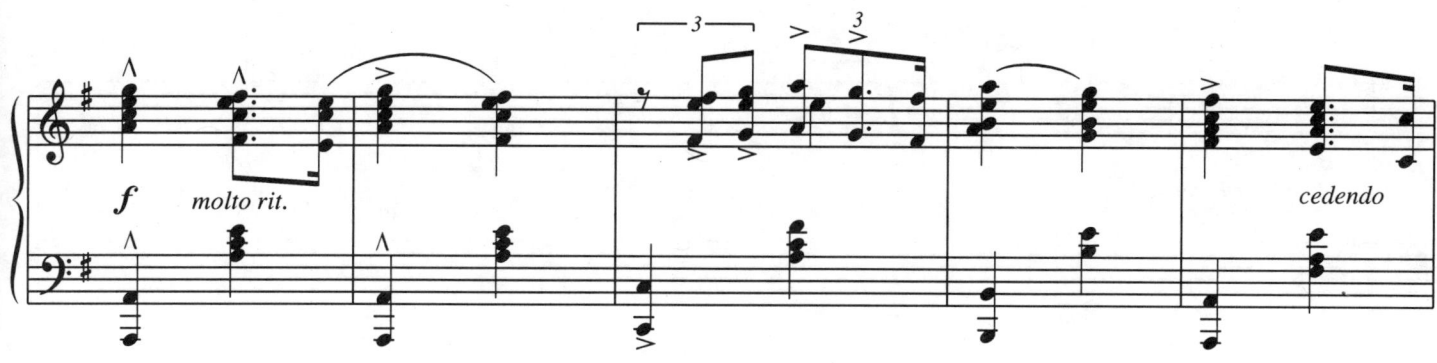

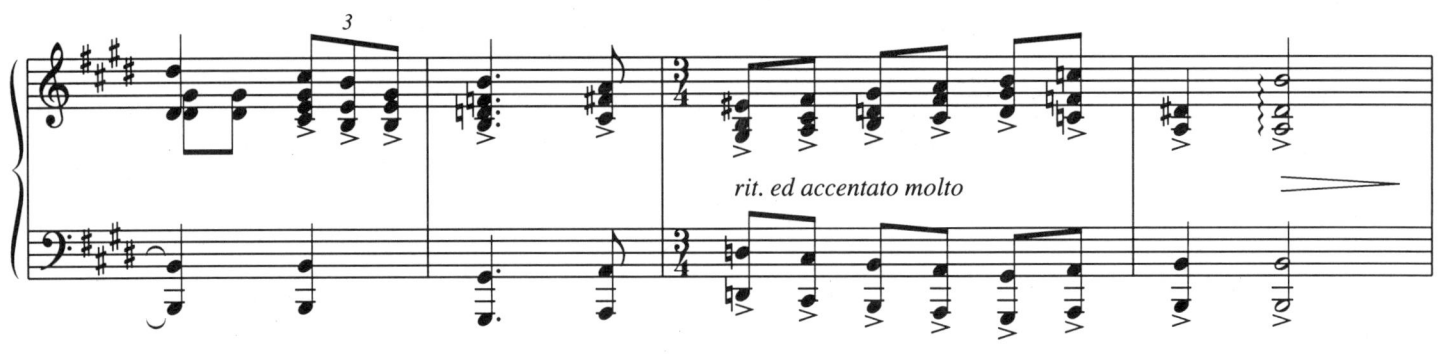
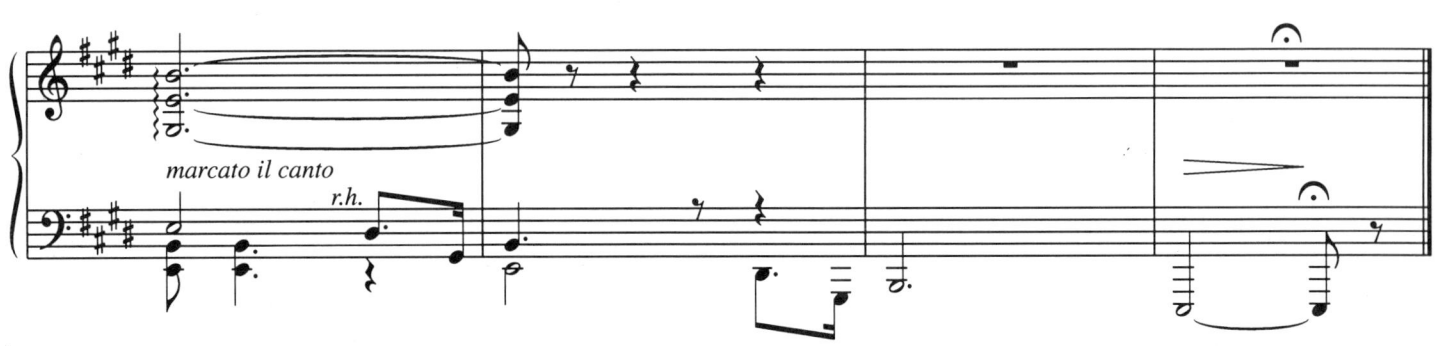

Timeless Favorites Arranged for Piano Solo — Broadway ▼ Jazz ▼ Standards

George Gershwin Piano Solos
Bill Boyd
Intermediate
12 favorites, including: A Foggy Day • I Got Plenty O' Nuttin' • Let's Call The Whole Thing Off • Nice Work If You Can Get It • Summertime • They Can't Take That Away From Me • more.
00359890 / $7.95

Cole Porter Piano Solos
Bill Boyd
Intermediate
11 of his best, including: Begin The Beguine • I Get A Kick Out Of You • I Love You • In The Still Of The Night • It's Delovely • and more.
00360840 / $7.95

Variations For Piano
Andrew Lloyd Webber
Upper Intermediate
This book represents an arrangement for the solo pianist of selected variations on the theme of Paganini's "A Minor Caprice." Great care has been taken to be faithful to the original score. ("Variations" served as the music for the "Dance" half of the Broadway show *Song And Dance*.)
00361447 / $9.95

Broadway Overtures For Piano Volumes 1 & 2
Advanced
Each Broadway Overture volume is a collection of some of the greatest overtures and entr'actes (music played before the 2nd or 3rd act of a show) ever to be heard, each one a piano reduction of the authentic material. The selections included in this two-volume set were chosen particularly for playability and overall appeal. This is the first major collection of Broadway overtures ever offered. In the past, a person would have had to purchase the vocal scores for each of these shows in order to have all of the overtures, making these collections an excellent value.

Volume 1
11 selections: Babes In Arms • Camelot • Carousel • The Fantasticks • Gypsy • Kiss Me Kate • My Fair Lady • Oklahoma! • On Your Toes • Paint Your Wagon • South Pacific.
00359441 / $9.95

Volume 2
14 selections: Camelot • Can Can • A Funny Thing Happened On The Way To The Forum • Funny Girl • The King And I • Kismet • Lost In The Stars • Oklahoma! • On A Clear Day You Can See Forever • On Your Toes • Paint Your Wagon • Show Boat • The Sound Of Music • South Pacific.
00359442 / $9.95

Rodgers & Hammerstein Piano Solos
Bill Boyd
Upper Intermediate
12 songs: Edelweiss • If I Loved You • Oh What A Beautiful Morning • The Sound Of Music • We Kiss In A Shadow.
00240825 / $9.95

Prices, contents, and availability subject to change without notice.

Jazz Standards Playin' Jazz Series
Bill Boyd
Easy
14 favorites, carefully arranged to preserve the jazz styling of each song. Includes: All Of Me • In The Mood • My Funny Valentine • They Can't Take That Away From Me • and more.
00365139 / $6.95

Swingtime Favorites Playin' Jazz Series
Bill Boyd
Easy
Part of the Playin' Jazz Series, this book includes 13 favorite "swing" tunes, carefully arranged to preserve the styling of each song. Includes: Ain't Misbehavin' • Cry Me A River • The Lady Is A Tramp • and more.
00366235 / $6.95

20 Ragtime Jazz Classics For Piano
Advanced
20 classics arranged as piano solos for the advanced player, including: Maple Leaf Rag • Chromatic Rag • The Entertainer • Evergreen Rag • Champagne Rag • and more!
00490247 / $9.95

Jazz On Broadway Playin' Jazz Series
Bill Boyd
Easy
12 great show tunes, including: Hello Young Lovers • I've Grown Accustomed To Her Face • People • Summertime • more.
00365135 / $6.95

For more information see your local music dealer or contact...

Hal Leonard Publishing Corporation
7777 West Bluemound Road P.O. Box 13819 Milwaukee, WI 53213